Fragility

Fragility
A History of Plaster

Alain Corbin

Translated by Helen Morrison

polity

Originally published as *Fragilitas. Le plâtre et l'histoire de France* © 2023 by
Éditions Plon, un Département de Place des Editeurs, Paris

This English translation © Polity Press, 2025

Polity Press
65 Bridge Street
Cambridge CB2 1UR, UK

Polity Press
111 River Street
Hoboken, NJ 07030, USA

ISBN-13: 978-1-5095-6594-8 – hardback
ISBN-13: 978-1-5095-6595-5 – paperback

A catalogue record for this book is available from the British Library.

Library of Congress Control Number: 2024948714

Typeset in 11 on 14 pt Sabon LT Pro
by Cheshire Typesetting Ltd, Cuddington, Cheshire
Printed and bound in Great Britain by CPI Group (UK) Ltd, Croydon

The publisher has used its best endeavours to ensure that the URLs for external
websites referred to in this book are correct and active at the time of going to
press. However, the publisher has no responsibility for the websites and can
make no guarantee that a site will remain live or that the content is or will remain
appropriate.

Every effort has been made to trace all copyright holders, but if any have been
overlooked the publisher will be pleased to include any necessary credits in any
subsequent reprint or edition.

For further information on Polity, visit our website:
politybooks.com

Our fathers had a Paris of stone
– our children will have a Paris of plaster.

Victor Hugo, *The Hunchback of Notre-Dame*, 1833

Contents

Acknowledgements

Without the active participation of my friend Professor Jacques Hentraye, this book would not have been possible.

My deepest thanks go to Sylvie Le Dantec, who was the first person to see and read this text.

History: from stone to plastic

In the past, the very first chapter of primary school 'history' textbooks – and, by the same token, the very first lesson – was dedicated to prehistoric times. Teachers introduced their pupils to two key concepts. The first of these was the sheer length of this period during which man concentrated his attention on survival and on overcoming the many challenges of existence. The second concerned the key elements of this timeline, with the emphasis placed much more on materials and techniques, rather than on what would, at a later stage, be referred to as 'lifestyle'. The past was presented in terms of chrononyms which referred to the dominant material of that time: the Stone Age (initially with crudely cut stone tools and later more refined ones made of polished stone), the Bronze Age, the Iron Age, etc., right until the Neolithic Age, also referred to as the New Stone Age.

The second lesson focused on the birth of history, linked to the invention and practice of many different writing systems and the splendour of the Babylonian and Egyptian civilizations, amongst others. In order to mark this abrupt change, this starting point of history, chrononyms referring to materials were no longer used. They have subsequently never reappeared, except perhaps in our imaginations, as demonstrated by the fascination exerted by the standing stones of Carnac or Stonehenge.

Yet materials have continued to exert a subtle influence on our perception of time. The solidity of Carrara marble, sculpted notably by Michelangelo, as well as its dazzling brightness, were closely associated with the period referred to by Michelet as the Renaissance, while the blackness of coal left its mark on the collective imagination of the English in the first decades of the nineteenth century.

But the situation was to become even clearer in subsequent years when the metal girder succeeded in imposing itself on the public mind to such an extent that it could indeed be regarded as a material chrononym in its own right, symbolizing, between 1860 and 1945, solidity, strength and even a kind of brute force in the construction of buildings, market halls and metal bridges, as well as in the manufacture of arms. Its appeal to the collective imagination reached a peak with the huge crowds of tourists flocking to see the Eiffel Tower during the Paris Exposition of 1889.

From 1945 onwards, a new material – in the form of plastic – took centre stage, and this too could be regarded as a chrononym. On the eve of the Second World War, when my brother and I played together, most of our games revolved around Meccano, an activity which represented the advent of the metal girder in the realm of children's toys. Subsequently, everything changed with the advent of nylon stockings, neon lighting and then, between 1950 and 1970, the invasion of an omnipresent plastic, all of which marked a revolution in the presence and use of materials in our lives. Focusing their attention on the village of Plozévet in Brittany, Edgar Morin and his skilful team of researchers drew attention to a phenomenon which was soon to be observed across all rural areas.[1] Farmers, many craftsmen, and even the middle classes threw away, burnt or confined to outhouses any kitchen items made of wood, with the result that tables, sideboards and dressers found themselves relegated to the scrap heap along with traditional bedroom wardrobes, all of them destined to be replaced by equivalent items very often made of formica. In a great many interiors, plastic now reigned supreme.

In a relatively short space of time, 'Tupperware parties', initially intended to promote plastic containers of all shapes and sizes, resulted in a hitherto unknown form of social activity which was essentially the preserve of women. Too little attention has been paid to this innovation, which ended up modifying working practices, creating free time and reconfiguring conversations between women, and which was undoubtedly a factor in their emancipation.

But if we delve a little deeper into the details, there is yet more to be discovered. Bags – large and small; packaging materials, previously in the form of paper, cardboard or natural textile; bottles; glass carafes; the metal cutlery which was our grandmothers' pride and joy – all soon began to be manufactured exclusively in plastic. At the end of the meal, all the cutlery, glasses, plates and dishes could be thrown away – everything was now disposable. The glory of plastic was demonstrated with considerable fanfare during the opening ceremonies of the vast factories destined to produce it by the thousands of tons.

At a much later stage, it became apparent that these same objects were invading rivers, forests, coastlines and oceans and that their indestructible nature in fact represented a serious threat – that even fish had been affected. Worse still, people had been ingesting and inhaling minuscule elements of plastic. From that time onwards, our bodies all contained plastic in some form or another. War on plastic was therefore declared and it would be by no means absurd to refer to the period extending from 1945 to 2022 as the age of plastic, pending the advent of a new material chrononym ... and, with the omnipresence of fibre, there is certainly no shortage of candidates in our present time.

From the same perspective, we have come to regard the period extending from 1815 to 1855 in France as the reign of plaster, with this material acting as a chrononym in its own right and thereby transforming the decades in question into a half-century of plaster.

It remains now to justify this hypothesis and to demonstrate the significance of this material, which during that period was becoming ever more invasive. It was a material with rich potential in agriculture and construction, in the amalgamation of all manner of debris, in art, in private and sentimental life, in medicine and even as a reflection of the different political regimes, which resemble a series of moulds like those used for plaster casts. In addition, we should not forget that plaster in a sense also suggests the direction taken by history, the appeal of eclecticism, the fascination with the discontinuity of time and, in brief, the sense of a flawed existence. Plaster

– symbol of the hollow, the crumbling, the ephemeral, the transient and the vulgar – is therefore the material that best defines the first half of the nineteenth century.

1

The half-century of plaster

What effect, whether physical or psychological, did the omnipresence of plaster have on people in France in the first part of the nineteenth century? In one of his *Propos*, the philosopher Alain[1] briefly turned his attention to this subject: 'Plaster is ugly because it can take on any form whatsoever. The most beautiful form, as everyone knows, loses much from this over-lenient material.'[2] It is a material, therefore, with connotations of pretence and sham.

Plaster is a friable material which produces a white dust. Mixed with water, it becomes malleable. It is not easy to handle and must be mixed with care. Plastering requires a certain level of technical skills if the smoothly polished surface and the dazzling white finish characteristic of this elusive material are to be successfully achieved.

Plaster is also used to stick items together, for distempering and coating surfaces and even for colouring. Covering a facade with plaster is a way of protecting it. Replastering strengthens the walls of a dwelling or a monument, filling in any cracks which have appeared. Plaster is useful when it comes to reassembling and sticking together scattered fragments. It allows remnants of debris to be stuck back together.

Most importantly, it readily lends itself to being moulded on a variety of different supports and dries rapidly. Consequently, as we shall see, the use of plaster for making casts has become a fundamental and widely used technique, whether for making casts of ancient works of art or for casting from nature, either to create a death mask or in the process of life-casting the human body or a fragment of it. Not surprisingly, medicine lost no time in adopting this technique.

Because of its fragile nature, plaster also lends itself to the production of ephemeral objects, easily broken and of little value. It is intrinsically associated with debris, with the production of fakes. It lends itself to jumble, to 'the bric-à-brac confraternity'[3] and, because of its modest cost, to the accumulation of objects. In the eyes of cultured individuals – whether we think of Balzac, Hugo or, even more pertinently, of Flaubert – it is the very epitome of all that is vulgar and symbolizes ugliness, and even stupidity. It is an object of disparagement.

The link between plaster and health is a complex one. On the one hand, plaster transforms hovels into more wholesome places and purifies 'domestic atmospheres'.[4] On the other hand, the strong smell emanating from fresh plaster was a source of anxiety. This explains why the hygienists of the first half of the nineteenth century recommended avoiding newly plastered surfaces and why being the first occupants in buildings with freshly plastered walls and 'wiping down the fresh plaster'[5] with your clothes was considered to be dangerous. Doctors advised landlords to rent such properties to prostitutes or to the poor for the first few months after the plaster had been applied. An inevitable tension reared its head in any discussions touching on the sanitizing qualities of plaster and on its dangerous odour.

It was, however – and this is worth emphasizing – plaster casts, and in particular those made from ancient masterpieces, that really contributed to the splendour and the importance of plaster during this period. Official bodies were eager to obtain such casts. In drawing schools, which were proliferating rapidly at the time, plaster casts were used as teaching aids and often served as models. In the studios of the greatest artists and the most famous sculptors, the walls and shelves were cluttered with them and some artists made casts of their models directly from life.

Plaster also lent itself to the decoration of surfaces – in particular, of monuments – and, as a result, it served to commemorate the past, to slow down innovation and to encourage eclecticism.

As a material, it symbolized a sense of a flawed existence, of uncertainty, traits stemming essentially from its crumbling nature, its absence of depth, its skin-like consistency and, once again, its associations with the fake, with debris and clutter.

Looked at from a different perspective, at the time in question, plaster – like marble in the past – had become a temporal symbol in a multiplicity of different ways, representing the hollow, the era of debris. On this point, specialists in literary history have frequently cited Alfred de Musset. Works in plaster, allegories of the transient, are the illustrations of a phantom century, a time lacking any cohesion and incapable of producing any enduring creations – in architecture, or in any other field.

During the same period, plaster casts served as a reminder and an evocation of past eras which they were capable of bringing back to life. They helped to recapture the past and were often closely associated with a penchant for history, considered so important at that time. Was this not, after all, the era of the great historians, of Augustin Thierry, of Thiers, of Guizot and of Michelet? Plaster highlights the evidence of the discontinuity of the time, it is in tune with changes in regimes of historicity.[6] In this time of uncertainty, with the triumph of the ephemeral and short-lived, and before the solidity of the metal girder finally succeeded in imposing itself, plaster was foremost in people's minds. It enabled different eras to be blended together and depicted in architecture, sculpture and painting. The creation of museums and the restoration of buildings, particularly those dating from the Middle Ages, were the most obvious manifestations of this new relationship with time.

This growing awareness of the discontinuity of time, this passion for history – and it is worth noting that many of the great names in politics at that time were indeed historians (Thiers, Guizot, Lamartine, Napoleon III) – echoes the popular obsession with plaster. Political history at the time was simply a succession of short-lived regimes whose lack of solidity stemmed from the fact that they were merely moulded on past regimes. This process is particularly obvious under the July Monarchy with the repatriation of Napoleon's ashes and the strenuous efforts made by Louis-Philippe I to put history centre stage.

The rapidity with which these regimes followed on from each other – five in fifty-two years – contrasts with the stability of the previous reign but, on the other hand, perfectly reflects the turmoil and upheaval of the Revolution. This political moulding process has a hollow ring about it. It echoes the dominant eclecticism and, in a sense, the poetry of ruins and debris epitomized in the Bastille elephant featured in Victor Hugo's novel *Les Misérables*.[7]

As a result of its ubiquity and its many different uses, plaster symbolizes the present but at the same time is a reminder of the past and a means of restoring former times. During that period, the obsessive fear of replication seems to have been more powerful than the inevitable progress decreed by the Republic. This can be seen in action in the pessimism of numerous writers, such as Musset, Balzac and Flaubert. These deplored the scarcity of genuinely new monuments and the structural modifications made to existing ones, and they lamented the shift from solidity and the enduring nature of stone to the fragility of the all-triumphant and vulgar plaster.

In 1831, writing about Paris, Victor Hugo was already lamenting: 'Our fathers had a Paris of stone – our children will have a Paris of plaster.'[8] Little could he know that this would be followed by the era of steel and glass.

2

Plaster houses and poverty

The importance of plaster during the period covered in this book stems in part from its frequent use in constructions destined only to be short-lived. Generally speaking, as François Hartog emphasizes, plaster symbolizes an era 'when buildings stopped aspiring to durability'.[1] The link between plaster and poverty was therefore an obvious one, as has been clearly illustrated by, amongst others, Jacques Hantraye, specialist in the history of plaster, or Vincent Farion, who portrays it as the symbol of poverty and false luxury.

On this subject, let us turn our attention again to something that has only been touched on briefly so far. The need to 'wipe down the fresh plaster'[2] was a notion widely espoused at the time. So, for example, in his manual for architects and stonemasons, Morel, a former building inspector, emphasized the need to 'wipe down the fresh plaster' in the interiors of any recently constructed buildings during an entire summer and winter.[3] In traditional construction methods, the general consensus was that plaster should be left to dry for a period of several months, with rooms being kept well ventilated and heated for an extended period.

Such practices are significant. They have resulted in an association between plaster, a generally disparaged material, and poverty. 'When it is not possible to dry plaster artificially', wrote Jacques Hantraye, 'properties are let initially to the poor, in exchange for a favourable rent', and if necessary to courtesans or 'kept women', or to 'registered'[4] prostitutes. In 1852, at the end of the period we are focusing on, a certain Dr Medink added workers from the wholesale trade to this list.[5]

Such stipulations resulted in significant numbers of short-term tenants in new buildings. According to Jacques Hantraye, the large numbers of female tenants initially installed in new Parisian buildings in order to accelerate the drying out of the fresh plaster was a reflection of the social transformations and changes in the construction industry during the first half of the nineteenth century. Balzac described the Paris of that period in his novel *History of the Thirteen*:

> During that period Paris had a building mania. Accordingly, at that moment, the whole population was demolishing or rebuilding something or other, somehow or other. Few were the streets free from scaffolding, with its long poles, its stocks of plank hitched on to crosspieces and hoisted on putlogs from storey to storey: frail constructions trembling under the feet of the masons but strengthened with ropework, white all over with plaster.[6]

In 1844, in *A Harlot High and Low*, Balzac pointed out the proliferation of temporary constructions, in particular those built by smallholders in areas on the outskirts of Paris. 'The plaster and rubble-stone so abundant in Nanterre, where the surrounding district is full of open quarries, had been, as they commonly are on the outskirts of Paris, made use of in haste and without the least architectural consideration.'[7] In his novels, Balzac frequently draws attention to the ugliness of the plaster facades masquerading as stone.

However, in the countryside around Paris, these miserable houses are not the only target of Balzac's scorn. Near them, 'plaster palaces' had been erected, along with what he describes as 'papier-mâché ornaments'.[8]

In the capital itself, as in a great many other French towns and cities, plaster was closely associated with poverty. In modern Paris, according to the author of *Le Père Goriot*, noble buildings are 'intermingled with filthy and shameful plaster constructions'. So, for example, on the Boulevard des Italiens, 'plaster, short-lived ornaments, everything is makeshift and pitiful'.[9] There, 'insubstantial houses with slender pillars and skimped porticoes' are a symbol of the Parisian *nouveaux riches*.[10]

But the link between plaster and poverty can be seen even more clearly in other parts of the capital. In 'An episode under the Terror', Balzac describes one of the houses typical of the area around the Faubourg Saint-Martin: 'The tottering hovel, built of porous stone in rough blocks, was coated with yellow plaster much cracked and looked ready to fall before a gust of wind.'[11]

Between the slopes of Montmartre and the higher ground of Montrouge stretched 'a valley full of plastered architecture crumbling to swift decay'.[12] Everywhere, the walls were 'streaked with black and yellow lines left by the rain on the stucco of Paris'.[13]

The interior of these dwellings was entirely in keeping with their external appearance. Balzac describes the thinness of 'partitions made of lath and plaster'[14] in the Rue Corneille, and these were by no means unusual. In Père Goriot's house, 'the paper had peeled in strips from the damp wall, showing the plaster yellow with smoke and age'.[15]

Could the omnipresence of this material with its association with poverty, so frequently described in Balzac's work, be in reality no more than the product of a novelist's imagination? We should of course be wary of taking at face value what may perhaps have been nothing more than a device to ensure coherence in a fictional context. Yet what we read in Balzac's novels, published for the most part between 1830 and 1850, is in fact supported by so much evidence, so many descriptions and so many written texts from outside the domain of fiction that it seems appropriate to turn to the novelist's work for a vivid depiction of the significance, and all-pervading presence, of plaster in the construction of buildings during this period.

The list of the various technical applications of plaster for anyone interested in building at that time demonstrates the rich variety of types of plaster available to them. The industrialists of that period were producing a whole range of plasters designed for moulding or for fertilizing agricultural land. In his article, Vincent Farion enthusiastically lists the range of plasters on offer: 'alabaster, mineral white [. . .] white plaster, grey plaster and even red plaster'.[16] In most cases, however, it was the sheer whiteness of this material that was particularly appreciated.

In the nineteenth century, the frequent use of plaster in major structural work also became widespread in the 'finishing work' of new buildings, where it was used for rendering walls and ceilings, and for decorative ornamentation in the form of mouldings or ceiling roses, all of which involved plaster work. Gradually, plaster blocks came to be widely used for internal partitions. Specialized workers were trained to produce this new material in the context of a growing enthusiasm for 'decorative mouldings'.

At the end of this period, when the demand for Hausmann-style buildings was at its peak, plaster, stucco, and then staff, which became popular during the 1860s, were all used in the decoration of both facades and living rooms. In particular, plastering inner walls and ceilings gave interiors that smooth finish, that clean appearance, that guarantee of reassuring solidity – and therefore security – which ultimately enabled private life to flourish amongst elite circles.

3

Restoring ancient monuments

It was not until the July Monarchy that the term 'restoration' came into regular usage. Prior to that point, in the wake of the large-scale destruction triggered not only by the Revolution but also by the subsequent Restoration, the upkeep of monuments had amounted to little more than preventing them from deteriorating, or even collapsing altogether. On some occasions that process was seen as an opportunity for a little embellishment.

This somewhat hasty approach, in which plaster played a major role, provoked the wrath of Victor Hugo during the course of his various journeys around France. In the town of Abbeville, he was delighted to see a beautiful abbey being repaired, but bemoaned the fact that the restoration work was being clumsily executed. The town hall of Arras, which dates from the time of Louis XIII, was a magnificent building:

> The facade would be admirable if only the local architects had not taken it upon themselves to improve it, with the result that it resembles the gothic décor from the old

Théatre de l'Ambigu-Comique.[1] Now they are restoring the bell tower. No doubt they will give this poor building a similar treatment!

In 1837, having just been made a member of the Comité des Monuments, Hugo expressed his regret that so many buildings had been badly restored, 'neglected, scratched or distempered'. He claimed to have fled from Cambrai, which he described as a 'marvel of boredom'.[2]

In almost all these restoration projects, plaster proved to be the preferred material, even if Victor Hugo generally avoids mentioning it specifically, except when with reference to 'distemper'. It is another matter altogether, however, when he directs his anger towards what he regarded as counterfeit practices, those 'inappropriate' restorations which ended up spoiling the monuments concerned. The worst example of this, in his view, was to be found in Épernay. The town's third church – 'the existing church, under the aegis of the worthy merchant Poterlet-Galichet' – is described as a *hideous plaster construction*, crude, white and heavy, with triglyphs supporting the archivolts'. We know that this building, a complex construction and in danger of complete collapse, had undergone major repairs – the very ones so fiercely denigrated by Hugo – that were completed in 1833. As for the remains of the two previous churches, they fared little better: 'The stained-glass windows and the portal are, of course, marooned and trapped in the awful plaster work of the new church.'[3]

In Chalon-sur-Saône, the poet gave vent to his anger, declaring: 'the church is filthy'; the sculptures, dating from the time of Francis I, are 'daubed' in yellow distemper, all the ribs in the vaulting are smothered in paint.[4]

As early as 1834, during his travels through Normandy, he was saddened to see the beautiful little Romanesque church near Ribaye 'plastered and spoiled'.[5]

It is worth pointing out that, according to specialists on Victor Hugo, the poet's ire was, at this period in his life, exacerbated by his hostility towards the July Monarchy. Nevertheless, plaster and distemper are particular targets in his litany of hates. This list reflects the pain and anger he felt when faced with the incapacity of his era to restore the beauties of the past, and its failure to engage in any genuine architectural creation. Plaster, more than any of this, epitomizes his frustration.

Let us briefly turn our back on Victor Hugo's outpourings of anger and focus our attention instead on the different stages that have marked the role of plaster in the conservation and restoration of monuments. Up until the last decade of the July Monarchy, sometimes referred to as the 'age of prosthetics',[6] plaster had not played any very significant role in restoration and conservation work. Leaving a religious work incomplete would, during the period in question, have been regarded as sacrilegious, and this attitude, as Geneviève Bresc-Bautier writes, was a factor in both conservation and deterioration, 'not to mention the multiple layers of paint and the successive removal of parts of statues'.[7] It was a time when strenuous efforts were made 'to keep intact the bodies of any individuals represented in sculpture, come what may, particularly with regard to any symbolic objects they might be holding'. There was considerable reluctance to leave an ancient artwork 'in its existing state' when it was perceived to be in any way diminished, or 'deprived of its fundamental elements'. Consequently, in the name of respect for art, 'it was considered acceptable to complete, to "restore" and even "embellish"'[8] any such pieces. All of this resulted in what amounted to an extensive programme of reworking and replacement.

During the period in question, the damaged statue would be taken down and replaced by a new one, created from scratch using substitute materials and without too much attention being paid to authenticity, an attitude which provoked an outcry amongst scholars devoted to the Middle Ages. It is certainly true that these sculptures, often carved out of a totally different material from the original, bore little resemblance to the initial work. The same scenario was played out at Saint-Denis, Paris, Senlis and Amiens.

From 1838 onwards, everything changed.[9] The prominent figures in restoration began to use plaster casts – which involved making an impression of the original – particularly in the case of medieval monuments. Plaster became an essential material, both for reproducing existing statues and as a working medium in its own right. The process of taking a plaster cast was an 'easy and inexpensive way of reproducing an object in the minutest detail',[10] without the need to sculpt copies or to erect models on site.

From 1838 to 1850, plaster therefore became the material of choice, prior to the age of co-creation (see below). In 1838, Jean-Baptiste-Antoine Lassus, the architect responsible for the restoration of the main portal of the church of Saint-Germain-l'Auxerrois, was determined to 'preserve the spirit of the existing structure', and plaster became a 'medium of transfer'[11] allowing the memory of the original to be conserved in three dimensions. Moreover, the destruction associated with the Revolution was such that a simple restoration on the basis of an exact copy was no longer possible. The construction site at Saint-Germain-l'Auxerrois created a precedent and attracted considerable numbers of architects and artists with a wide variety of skills, who would later promote Gothic, or so-called neo-Gothic, architecture.

From 1838, the restoration techniques used on the Saint-Germain site – and, in particular, experiments involving making casts of decorative elements of monuments in need of restoration – were expanding in scope. Plaster, previously neglected, began to assume a vital place. So, for example, in 1839, the sculptures of the church of La Couture, in Le Mans, were copied exactly from the still-intact existing statues, thanks to the technique of casting. From then on, the use of this technique was regarded as an essential element in any restoration programmes.

Members of learned societies were the first to welcome this use of mouldings and casts. They rightly saw this exact reproduction as a way of preserving the memory of monuments. Arcisse de Caumont, founder and president of the Société des antiquaires de Normandie, awarded subsidies to encourage the spread of these techniques. Thanks to the practice of casting, it became possible to produce duplicates of any works deemed to be fragile. Most importantly, this technique meant that a damaged or missing statue could be replaced by the copy of another and more prestigious one. In other words, casting techniques served to fill a gap, though with the risk that multiple copies of the most famous Gothic statues would end up on display in many different churches. The proliferation of copies of great works of art made possible as a result of this process continued to spread during the years 1850 to 1855, a period when the use of plaster was increasingly considered as an *ex nihilo* element of civic and religious ornamentation.

Gradually, the use of casts lent itself to an even more extraordinary practice, in which the process served to replace an original plaster sculpture with an exact copy except that this version was solid, new and copied in stone. This marked the start of the era of exact reproduction in stone, thanks to the technique of casting, advocated by, amongst others, Viollet-le-Duc.

In many places, the decision was made to replace missing statues by turning for inspiration to casts of existing statues, as was the case in Le Mans. Casting also made it easier to combine a number of different models. The famous facade of Notre-Dame Cathedral in Paris is an example of an unprecedented mix of old and new.[12] In 1842, when Viollet-le-Duc drew up his restoration plans, very little external decorative work remained intact at Notre-Dame, as much of it had been mutilated in the eighteenth century. The Revolution had seen the destruction of many statues, such as those in the Gallery of Kings and around the main portals. The architects therefore decided both to use casts to replicate previously existing statues and to create new ones.

During the same period, plaster casts began to be used as models for sculptors. As early as 1840, at Vézelay, Viollet-le-Duc had used 'original models which were then finished off in plaster'. In this mid nineteenth century, therefore, plaster was being used in an increasing number of ways, both in restoration and in creation – a phenomenon which would be reflected in the texture of political regimes, where innovation and creation coexisted with a process more akin to casting and moulding.

Let us return to the case of Viollet-le-Duc. In Vézelay, the architect had used a combination of moulds, casting and original creation.[13] In order to compensate for missing elements in the casting of the corbels, he came up with a drawing created from scratch which was then transposed first into plaster and then into stone. Because of its pliability, plaster, as Sophie Lagabrielle points out, lent itself to the trials and experiments normally associated with a creative approach. From the existing repertoire of models to the production of creative copies, a new process was being used, all centred around this white material. Whereas, before 1850, casting was used to produce a statue identical to the original in every detail, the production of a creative copy was widely seen as a way of adding the finishing touches to the work of the Middle Ages.

This concept of a 'creative copy' did not completely undermine the casting process. During the restoration of a monument, a variety of approaches could be used. This was the case at Notre-Dame in Paris where the restoration was inspired by a vision of an idealized fourteenth-century cathedral, with the sculptors drawing inspiration from plaster casts. Another example is the Chateau at Blois, where casts were made from part of the vestiges of the former castle, which were then used as a basis for its restoration. This explains how the presence of plaster came to play such a significant role in the flowering of neo-Gothic architecture.

This complex history of the preservation and then subsequent restoration of monuments resulted in a combined process of making moulds of any elements needing to be replaced – in other words, the practice of casting – and the production of authentic models to be used as the basis for creative copies. Without exception, from the beginning of the July Monarchy, plaster occupied a central role. It was one of the reasons why this material was such a crucial element in these multiple attempts to rediscover the past. Thanks to the subtle interplay of the hollow and the solid, of the ephemeral and the enduring, plaster was to play a real and symbolic role in shaping the historic concept of time.

4

Plaster: allegory of a phantom century

There can be little doubt that, at the beginning of the nineteenth century, the people of France moved into a new regime of historicity – or, in other words, into a different relationship with time. Indeed, in a well-known passage from his *Memoirs from beyond the Tomb*, François-René de Chateaubriand puts this change into words:

> I have found myself between two centuries as at the junction between two rivers; I have plunged into their troubled waters, regretfully leaving the ancient strand where I was born and swimming hopefully towards the unknown shores.[1]

In his recent book, François Hartog vividly portrays how perceptions of time were radically overturned.[2]

The immediate aftermath of the fall of Napoleon I heralded a new era in which ruins and debris featured prominently. There was an urgent need to reassemble the scattered fragments, and this extended even to the social sphere.[3] The nineteenth century is the first century to be named according to an ordinal calculation.

As the new century opened, many magnificent works of literature turned their attention to this new perception of time. In his novel *The Confession of a Child of the Century*, Alfred de Musset offers the most striking example of this, but Honoré de Balzac, Benjamin Constant and many others also voiced their suffering – or, at the very least, the sense of confusion – brought on by living in such uncertain times and finding themselves confronted on all sides by an accumulation of debris and ruins. These were the result of a number of factors, including the iconoclasm imposed by the revolutionaries, the destruction and repurposing of monuments previously owned by either the church or the nobility, and the sale of national assets that, more than anything else, contributed to this proliferation of rubble. The presence of this debris reflected the urgent need for construction materials and the unscrupulous activities of the so-called 'Bandes noires', groups of speculators who purchased ruins only to subsequently sell the stones as building materials.

This atmosphere of confusion, this proliferation of rubble and the unprecedented overturning of social status led initially to feelings of disorientation, anxiety and pessimism.[4]

Seeking to depict his era, Musset writes: 'in short the present century which separates the past from the future, which is no longer the one nor yet the other but is simultaneously both; and being in it we do not know, with every step we take, if we are stepping out on the seeds of the new or the rubble of the old'.[5] He goes on to portray the spirit of the century as an 'angel of the half-light' and describes how the young people of the time 'found it seated upon a bag of quicklime, full of bones, squeezed into the cloak of egoists, shivering with bone-eating cold. The anguish of death percolated into their souls at the sight of that spectre, which was half mummy and half foetus.'[6]

Standing in front of the rubble strewn across his field, a man 'awaits the coming of new stones for his new home'. But, 'When he is ready to dress the blocks and mix his mortar and stands pick in hand, arms bared for action, another man comes and tells him there is a shortage of stones and advises him to whitewash the ones he has, to make the best of things.'[7] Here, Musset is making a surreptitious reference to the need to resort to plaster.

Later in the book, Musset writes:

> Our century has no distinct style of its own. We have failed to stamp the seal of our age on our houses, our gardens, on anything at all. [. . .] We have flotsam from every century except our own, and that is something that has never been true of any other period in history. Eclecticism is our form of taste. We take whatever we find, this because it is beautiful, that because it is useful or because it is old or even because it is very ugly. *The upshot is that we live off leftovers, as if the end of the world were nigh.*[8]

We shall return to this subject later when we turn our attention to the profusion of plaster figures and clutter and 'the bric-à-brac confraternity' so familiar to Balzac's Cousin Pons.

In the most debauched areas of Paris, Musset observes the 'burning torches lighting up painted heads'. These are mere 'husks of women',[9] and, in this context, it is impossible not to think of those rebellious prostitutes who lived in the profoundest depths of urban poverty and who were given the nickname of the 'pierreuses' (the women of the stones) because they took refuge and plied their trade amongst the ruins and debris of the poorest districts, where plaster mingled with stone.

The nineteenth century was born in an atmosphere of confusion. No one succeeded better than the young Alfred de Musset in conveying this 'sense of a flawed existence'[10] that characterized the emerging century, in quest of its identity[11] yet at the same time haunted by a growing need to seek refuge in times gone by, whose solid nature seemed in stark contrast to this 'phantom century'. The popular French expression *essuyer les plâtres* (literally, 'to wipe down fresh plaster', but with its connotations of being the first to do something) sums this up perfectly. Musset was the first person to encapsulate in literature this sense of anxiety and pessimism born out of the fragility of an era which he had experienced intensely at first hand.

It is worth noting, however, that, from the outset, this 'phantom century' also triggered the pleasure of nostalgia – the sense of the past as a refuge, the enjoyment to be derived from ruins and from amassing fragments of debris and discarded junk.

Plaster can therefore be regarded as the perfect symbol for the opening years of this phantom century. We have already seen how it epitomized the fragility of construction, as well as, in some cases, its ugliness. Yet, at the same time, it can also be seen as a reflection of the desire to conserve, and even restore, the testimony of past centuries, whose sheer solidity transforms them into a storehouse of memories.

But there is more. Plaster was, at that time, regarded as a symbol of the ephemeral. Let us not forget that it was associated with the production of buildings erected in haste. Its fragility quickly became synonymous with the notion of vulgarity, and was consequently often the target of criticism. For a long time, plaster carried a suggestion of the hollow, as epitomized by the casts taken of ancient artworks and, gradually, by those taken of the human body, living or dead, and of all nature's creatures.

What other material could more vividly represent this emerging century, this indeterminate time frame, than plaster, the embodiment of the ephemeral, with its associations of vulgarity, of discarded debris and even of the hollow? As a material, it was capable of preserving, of restoring and of reproducing the solidity of past ages through their masterpieces. Its fluid nature could, furthermore, be seen to embody what is perhaps the very essence of this emerging century – in other words, that sense of 'a flawed existence' – and its pliability reflected and favoured eclecticism and combination.

Plaster, which lent itself so well to the Troubadour style, and later – indirectly – to the neo-Gothic, was undoubtedly a factor in the inability to create admirable, solid monuments capable of representing this period preceding the advent of the metal girder.

5

Plaster casts and the art of the hollow

In the period following the fall of the *Ancien Régime*, the casting of artworks and busts of famous people was widely practised.[1] The sculptor Houdon was the most famous of all the artists working in plaster at that time and in 1795, a few years after the end of the *Ancien Régime* – probably during the period when tombs were being desecrated – he cast the remains of Richelieu.

As early as the sixteenth century, Francis I had sent the painter and sculptor Primaticcio to Rome to supervise the casting in bronze of a number of famous works of antiquity and to bring back those that would form part of the collection to be displayed in the chateau at Fontainebleau. Since the reign of Louis XV, plaster casts had taken on a didactic role, in addition to that of contributing to the glory of the monarch. They became objects of study and were one of the fundamental elements of an academic education. During the Age of Enlightenment, casts of ancient statues were greatly prized and were collected by academies, artists and amateurs alike.

The Revolution led to a surge of interest in the casting of ancient masterpieces. In 1794, the National Convention created the Atelier de Moulage du Louvre (the Casting Workshop at the Louvre Museum), a prelude to the establishment of a vast collection spanning every historical period.

Already under the National Convention and the Directory, artists, painters and, in particular, sculptors were responsible for suggesting the list of works to be cast. So, for example, on 24 Frimaire in Year III (14 December 1794), a request was made for preliminary casts to be made of a number of ancient works, notably Bernini's *Sleeping Hermaphroditus*, the Medici *Venus* and the Borghese *Gladiator*. Later, under the Empire, casts were made in Paris of most of the masterpieces removed from Italy to France under the terms of the treaty of Tolentino. During the Restoration, the Comte de Forbin, curator of the Louvre Museum, was involved in some spectacular castings, notably those of the Parthenon marbles, brought back from Greece by Lord Elgin and housed in the British Museum.

In the context of this book, it is essential to understand that French artists were initially introduced to ancient masterpieces through casts – and indeed for those unable to travel to Rome, this was the only means of seeing such works. The directors of the Villa Medici, for their part, endeavoured to honour orders for casts made by teachers from Paris art schools.

In this context, the importance of the Casting Workshop at the Louvre Museum cannot be overemphasized.[2] Prior to this, practice in this field had been somewhat erratic in the city of Paris. On 13 Ventose Year II (3 March 1794), the corporation of casters published a vehement tract decrying the gradual decline in the quality of casts produced in the capital at a time when the study of drawing was a compulsory element of secondary education. This petition attracted the attention of the government.

On 24 Frimaire Year III (14 December 1794), the day the Louvre workshop opened its doors for the very first time, the temporary arts commission invited the artist François-Marie Neveu to oversee the production of forty hollow moulds of the most beautiful ancient statues. This first collection of studio moulds brought an end to the somewhat tentative period which had preceded this moment and marked the official recognition of the supreme importance of plaster and hollow moulds in the conception and practice of sculptural art. The moulders Getty and Michely were allocated the task of selecting the models best suited to promote the art of sculpture.

Let us turn our attention for a moment to the casting workshop at the Louvre Museum, which represents the very core of our subject – epitomizing, in other words, the importance of plaster in the art of this period. The Louvre workshop was to become the model for other moulding and casting museums and collections.[3] A few simple principles governed the use of plaster within the workshop, replicating those already set out in the *Encyclopédie* edited by Diderot and d'Alembert – notably, the division of labour, the different levels of specialization corresponding to the various stages of the process, and the finishing touches which were reserved for the attention of the workshop head. The daily working hours of these plaster workers were fixed, as were their wages. At the time the workshop first opened, a workshop manager earned 2,000 francs a year, and a labourer from 9 to 15 francs per day, supplemented with various advantages of a professional nature.

The Louvre workshop was by no means unique within the capital. Certain casters had acquired a monopoly on plaster reproductions. The majority of these had their premises in the Saint-Antoine district, within easy reach of the École des Beaux-Arts, and, subsequently, in the area around Montparnasse, and others had set up outside of Paris. Most of them specialized in producing plaster figures associated with a particular era or a specific genre, such as religious statuary or figurines representing well-known social or political subjects, etc. In short, plaster workshops proliferated in this first half of the nineteenth century. Trade in objects made from this material flourished. Street vendors crisscrossed the capital, their arms laden with statuettes, figurines or the death masks of famous men. In rural areas, identical objects were sold by hawkers and pedlars.

Inside the workshops where plaster was worked, techniques evolved between 1815 and 1860.[4] Nevertheless, even within the Louvre workshop itself, the most common technique remained what was generally referred to as 'piece mould casting'.

From 1844 onwards, thanks to a newly developed technique, gelatine began to be used in certain stages of the process. Staff, invented in 1857 by Eugène-Denis Arrondelle, did not come into use until after 1860.

In the course of this half-century, a deontology began to emerge that would contribute to improvements in the quality of the casting process.[5] Focus increasingly shifted to preserving the original and this gradually became a priority. A great many sculptures were damaged during the casting process with scratches caused by the spatulas or knives used to free the mould from the original work. Some items ended up getting broken as a result of the plaster expanding – not to mention marks, oil stains and a whole range of other unfortunate consequences often associated with the release agents.

In order to fully appreciate just how influential plaster had become, it is important to recognize the sheer scale of the plaster cast trade. The Louvre Museum workshop was at the very heart of this process.[6] Under the supervision of a specialized workforce, large quantities of casts were dispatched to drawing schools, museums and artists, as well as to art lovers and to various different industries. It should be pointed out that the plaster casts in question were relatively inexpensive.

All the drawing schools – and there were a great many of these at that time – as well as the art academies needed to obtain a supply of 'edition plasters', and most of them obtained these from the Louvre, where they were eligible for favourable terms.[7] Requests for casts were made by prominent figures within the city. Sixty of these were registered under the Restoration, with numbers dropping under the subsequent regime and then rising rapidly under the Second Empire.

In the drawing schools – and these numbered over a hundred in Paris during the first half of the nineteenth century, with many others located in other major French cities – the programme of study emphasized the use of 'cast drawing', where students were encouraged to work from plaster casts of fragments of the human body. Two activities took precedence. First of all, students were expected to copy statues, a method designed to ensure they learned the principles of ideal beauty. The choice of statues was generally confined to the most famous works of antiquity. Throughout the nineteenth century, therefore, drawing schools were largely responsible for defining notions of classical beauty, a situation which sometimes provoked a certain amount of criticism. In addition to this activity, plaster casts of body parts were used, in the form of replicas of heads, legs and even ears and noses.

Amongst the critics of these new practices, one particular protest stands out. This took place in 1827 and was organized by a group of Parisian students who refused to accept the predominance of the neoclassical doctrine. 'Plaster replicas of ancient statues were broken up and heads, hands, feet and legs were thrown out of the windows.'[8] Not a single plaster cast was spared, not even the *Venus de Milo*.

Such incidents aside, the omnipresence of plaster casts in artists' studios represents one of the most significant factors in the proliferation of this material during this first half of the nineteenth century. As is clear from a great many pictorial representations of this period, the presence of plaster is striking. Most artists accumulated a large number of plaster casts in their studios and workshops. These were used as models or as a source of inspiration. They reflected the tastes of individual artists. Certain collections, ranging from that belonging to Ingres to that of Gustave Moreau, epitomized the enduring nature of this practice.

But the presence of plaster in artists' studios and workshops was not simply confined to the collecting of casts and to creative copies based on these. Many artists, whether apprentices or masters, sculpted in plaster with a view to producing authentic works of art in this material. Throughout the course of the nineteenth century, plaster was used in the creation of many masterpieces, a process culminating in the work carried out in Rodin's studio.

During this period, the plaster cast was by no means regarded as inferior: 'it was perceived as distinct from its model, like a real, authentic and complete reproduction which differed from the original only in terms of the material used'.[9] The copy unconsciously became a substitute for its model and was regarded as an artwork in its own right, one that certain museums were proud to own. Some people were even of the opinion that plaster could enhance the way an original work was viewed.

Within the museums, which were rapidly increasing in number at the time, casts had become an indispensable element, an aesthetic and iconographic reference point. It is important to take account of this perception of plaster in order to fully understand the influence this material had on the people of that time.

In the Louvre Museum, which since its inauguration had been regarded as a centre of study, of instruction and of art history, casts played a highly significant role and a 'gallery of casts' was created in 1829. And there was also a collection of casts at the École des Beaux-Arts[10] where, for a considerable period of time, teaching was largely centred on plaster copies. The school even had its own casting workshop.

Nevertheless, even more than by its widespread use in casting workshops, in museums and in schools, the extent of the influence of plaster in this first half of the nineteenth century is vividly demonstrated by its encroachment into the most intimate realm of private life.

6

Immortalizing the dead in plaster

In this first half of the nineteenth century, plaster not only found its way into public spaces, museums and artists' studios but also took on a significant role in private life, which was becoming increasingly important. We must therefore consider the specific emotions associated with the plaster death masks created in order to perpetuate the memory of a lost one and focus our attention on the use of plaster in immortalizing death.[1]

Prior to the advent of photography, the most common way of conserving the memory of a deceased person was through painting, and sometimes sculpture. Yet the role of plaster in the commemorative domain is often neglected. Jules Janin, for example, describes how, in 1834, he witnessed pedlars selling coarse plaster masks representing Cuvier, Girodet, Casimir-Pierre Perier or Géricault, a practice he condemned as highly blasphemous.[2]

Since the time of the Renaissance, the casting of death masks had been a princely and sometimes bourgeois practice, and was the tradition in northern countries.

As an element of the *ars moriendi*, it was reintroduced in the context of the Jansenist movement. Casts were made of the faces of Angélique Arnaud and of Blaise Pascal, for example. The technique used for this process of casting faces is described in detail in the Diderot and d'Alembert *Encyclopédie*. The very end of the eighteenth century saw a major revival of the death mask in two main arenas. In Germany, during the *Sturm und Drang* era, creating the death mask of a dead artist became part of a veritable cult devoted to musicians, poets and literary geniuses. The masks of Lessing (1781), Schiller (1805), Haydn (1809), Weber (1826) and, most important of all, Beethoven (1837) were amongst the most famous and were widely available during this period, when the face of the dead person was believed to reflect the soul and genius of the deceased.

Goethe regarded this practice with scepticism and insisted that death was a 'very poor portrait painter'. Nevertheless, he owned and displayed in his own home a death mask of Schiller. Furthermore, in 1807, and then in 1816 – aged respectively fifty-nine and sixty-seven – he had live casts made of his own face. On his death, at the age of eighty-three in 1832, a new mask was created.

As for Beethoven, in 1812, at the age of thirty-six, he had already had a cast made of his face. On his death in 1827, the impression of his face proved quite difficult to capture, but the result nevertheless met with enormous success. And Napoleon's death mask – a subject we shall be returning to – ended up being sold in record numbers.[3]

In France, during the Revolution, the guillotine led to the modification of certain practices but also to an increased interest in impressions taken from the faces of the dead. This was because the machine, by its very nature, focused attention on the head. Marie Grassholer took impressions of the decapitated heads and faces of political figures – including those of Desmoulins, d'Hébert, Danton and, probably, Robespierre – but this is of little relevance here since she used wax rather than plaster. For the same reason, the many engravings of decapitated heads – notably that of Louis XVI – examples of which proliferated during the Terror, fall outside the scope of this study.[4]

During the first half of the nineteenth century, what did people do with a death mask? It could be offered as a gift to a friend or, in the case of the mask of a loved one, placed on display in the living room or bedroom, either inside a display cabinet or under a simple glass dome, transforming it into a private shrine. Often – and this rapidly became a fashion – the mask was hung on a wall in order to avoid laying it flat. Sometimes the death mask was placed on a cushion, alongside figurines and various plaster ornaments. All these practices reinforced the presence of this material in aristocratic and bourgeois interiors. In these circles, the appeal of death masks ended up transforming certain interiors into what amounted to museums of the dead. One of the advantages of the death mask was that it could easily be carried when travelling.

In order to fully understand both what has previously been said and what is to follow, it is important to remember that in the nineteenth century looking at a dead body was not considered shocking – even in the presence of a large number of relatives and friends. We must not forget that in Paris bodies recovered by the police in the streets or along the banks of the river Seine were displayed in the morgue so that members of the public could identify them.[5] Indeed, a visit to the morgue might well form part of a Sunday afternoon stroll.

How was a death mask made?[6] The person making the mould rarely worked alone. He or she was generally accompanied and assisted by an apprentice. Sometimes, in the more elite circles, a sculptor, chosen by the family, would also be present to give advice to those engaged in making the mould, perhaps in the hope of being chosen to create a sculpture of the deceased which might at a later stage be commissioned by the family.

Throughout the period we are focusing on here, successive editions of the *Manuels Roret*[7] gave detailed instructions on how to handle the plaster during the process of moulding a death mask. The procedure, it should be noted, could be carried out in the presence of family members and friends gathered around the death bed. Gustave Flaubert described his anguish on witnessing the moulding of the death mask of Caroline, his beloved sister, on the day after her death. He wrote on the subject 'I shall have her hand and her face. I shall ask Pradier to make me her bust and will put it in my room.'[8]

First of all, the dead body was laid out horizontally. Then the mould maker or his apprentice would grease the skin, the roots of the hair, the eyebrows and the eyelashes. In the case of a man, the face was usually shaved. In addition, the hair could also be covered with a strip of cloth.

During the second stage of the process, the plaster was mixed with warm water and left until it began to harden. It could then be applied with a paintbrush.

Fragility

The procedure needed to be carried out as quickly as possible after death, before the onset of rigor mortis. Where necessary, if the cheeks had already become too hollow, they could be packed back into shape with oakum, though care needed to be taken not to alter the physiognomy of the deceased. With this in mind, memories gathered from those close to the dead person could prove extremely useful, since it was not uncommon for the weight and warmth of the plaster to alter the features after death.

The third stage, during which the mask was removed, carried the most risks. 'The plaster comes away in a solid block', states the *Manuel Roret*, but it is possible to 'open it from the middle into two halves by pulling on a wire previously inserted into the plaster'. If the mask was to include the ears, the process was more complicated and this explains why many mould makers chose to avoid this operation.

When this process was complete, the mask needed to be carefully cleaned in order to remove excess plaster and any traces of grease. All of this constituted what were referred to as the 'heavy' elements of the moulding process. In cases where the mould maker was accompanied by a sculptor, these tasks would be assumed by the latter. As a skilled artist, the sculptor added or removed plaster and smoothed out any roughness so as to attenuate the crude nature of the casting process. If necessary, the physical defects of the deceased could be effaced or the hair retouched. All of this, in the majority of cases, was done in response to requests from family members, who wanted the mask to bear as close a resemblance as possible to the physiognomy of the deceased during his or her lifetime.

The distribution of certain death masks provoked an intense emotional response amongst the general public. The most frequently cited example of this phenomenon was the mask of the painter Théodore Géricault.[9] Many people, including Eugène Delacroix, were deeply moved by this relic. It was said that the young painter, already famous, died of the 'pox' (syphilis). The emotional power of what was described as a 'remarkable casting', or as a 'remarkable plaster relic', was at that time reinforced by the fact that Géricault's death mask was to be found on display in a great many artists' studios. Over the course of several decades, it was the subject of many accounts and comments. In 1842, Charles Blanc wrote: 'There is scarcely a single artist's studio today where the plaster mask of Géricault is not to be found on display, an elongated mask, hollow-cheeked and bony and with a faint smile, the whole expression conveying a gentle irony and a sense of eternal regret.'[10]

The propensity of contemporary commentators to describe the emotions provoked by the contemplation of a plaster death mask serves to reinforce our understanding of the renewed importance this material had acquired in the popular sensibility.

But there is more to add when we turn our attention to the role of the death mask in the political sphere. We have already observed a similar phenomenon in relation to the guillotine, with the renewed fascination provoked by severed heads. But, in the context of death masks, it was that of Napoleon which proved to have the greatest impact of all, finding its way into even the poorest homes, where it was displayed alongside a handful of religious ornaments sold by travelling pedlars. Not without justification, Alain Pougetoux aptly subtitled his article on the subject, 'From relic to ornament'.[11]

During the morning of 7 May 1821, the day following the death of the deposed emperor, which had occurred at 7.50 in the evening, a mould for a death mask was made. The regular staff at Longwood[12] described the face of the deceased as thinner, certainly, but peaceful and 'astonishingly rejuvenated'. It was difficult to find good-quality plaster on the island of Saint Helena. However, Francis Burton, an English military doctor, was an expert at taking moulds. The ensuing cast was divided into two parts: the facial section, first of all, from the arch of the eyebrows to the tip of the chin, and then the rest of the skull, a section which was subsequently lost.

It was some considerable time later, in 1833, that François Antommarchi, who had been Napoleon's doctor on Saint Helena in the years before his death, set up a subscription in order to facilitate the wider distribution of the relic. The majority of the available masks were of plaster, others were in the form of bronze statues produced by skilled casters. The subscription met with immediate success, and over the following years the mask was reproduced in even greater numbers.

From that point onwards, artists began to draw inspiration from this example by depicting the plaster mask of the emperor in bourgeois interiors, but also – and in particular – in humbler settings. Antommarchi had foreseen the vast scale of the demand when he wrote, in 1833, in the text introducing the subscription: 'Everyone will have Napoleon's mask; and in a few years' time it will be found in every cottage, next to the cross on which our Saviour died.'

And that is exactly what happened. Napoleon's mask found its way into bourgeois interiors alongside various other objects – in particular, plaster statuettes like those which were produced in such numbers during the Romantic era. Every home had its plaster Napoleon.

7

Ornaments and figurines: plaster within the home

The first half of the nineteenth century was, as has already been observed, an era dominated by the ruins of the past, by cast-off detritus, by ill-assorted and incongruous objects, by clutter and, in some cases, by the fake and the vulgar. It was, above all, a period dominated by discontinuity, the very antithesis of solidity. All of this is epitomized and symbolized by plaster, that fragile and inexpensive substance, with its associations with the ephemeral – characteristics which also facilitated its widespread use and popularity across all levels of society.

We have seen how, in the field of construction, plaster reflected and encouraged a cumulative temporality or, in other words, the overlapping and blurring of historical periods.

Plaster, because of its malleability, also symbolizes the absence of any specific characteristics. In this sense, it typifies interiors full of a random accumulation of objects, often fragile and originating from a multiplicity of different sources.[1] This provides the inspiration for

44

the observations made by Raphael, the principal character in Balzac's *Peau de chagrin*, written in 1831. The omnipresence of plaster helps to reinforce the impression that France has been reduced to fragments, that it has adopted the chequered costume of Harlequin.

One of the manifestations of the pervasive presence of this material is evident in the new proliferation of ornaments and, in particular, of figurines. Such objects are easy to manufacture. They can be painted and, though fragile, are inexpensive to buy. During this period, such figurines typically depicted Jesus, the Virgin Mary and the saints and, in the south of France, the *santons* for the Christmas crib, as well as the heroes of French history such as Napoleon.

Figurines came in a great many guises. The fascination they exerted extended even to the different styles of dress they depicted, which were sometimes emulated – as was the case, for example, with the costumes of young troubadours seen on the streets of Paris. They also found their way into the work of writers at a time when interest in history was at a peak, in descriptions of characters representing a historical period. Musset, for example, observes: 'You walk along the street and see men with the kind of beards worn in the days of Henry III; others are clean-shaven, or have their hair cut as in the portraits of Raphael or in the time of Jesus Christ.'[2]

Nevertheless, the comical figurine, so often mentioned, remains that epitomized by Cousin Pons, the eponymous character of Balzac's novel published in 1847.[3]

Aged in his sixties, the protagonist belongs to that group of Parisians who:

Just go on wearing all the absurd fashions of their time. They seem to be personifications of a whole period [. . .] By maintaining in certain points of his attire an unconquerable fidelity to the modes of 1806, this passer-by reminded one of Imperial times without going so far as caricature. [. . .]

This thin, dried-up old man wore a nut-brown spencer over a greenish coat with white metal buttons! In 1844, meeting a man in a spencer made it seem as if Napoleon had deigned to come back to life for an hour or two.

Underneath all this was a rather picturesque figure with a 'fantastic face, squashed flat at each end like a pumpkin'. In his description of his clothes, Balzac refers to various past fashions, conjuring up the portrait of what can only be described as a veritable living figurine:

Over his shoes he had gaiters of Imperial Guard style [. . .] A huge white muslin cravat, with the showy kind of knot sported by lady-killers to allure the 'alluring women' of 1809, came up so far over his chin that his face seemed as if plunged into an abyss [. . .] so many relics of Empire fashion – were in keeping with the old-fashioned perfumes [. . .] which he exuded; so too was a curious trimness in the folds, and an indefinable dry meticulousness in the total effect, redolent of David's school and Jacob's dainty furniture.[4]

Balzac's detailed description helps to convey the range of emotions that a plaster figure was capable of triggering.

Prior to the 1830s, the French capital was already known for its pronounced taste for objects from the past, even those of no particular value, and these could be found piled high on the shelves of the junk shops Balzac referred to as 'the bric-à-brac confraternity'. These shops reflect the notion of debris we are exploring here, a debris often collected by junk dealers from chateaux either already in ruins or in the process of being demolished.

Unlike the junk dealers, antiquarians – a profession which made its first appearance in France in the 1830s – kept scrupulous and detailed inventories,[5] taking pride in distinguishing between and evaluating different historical periods. They were not interested in simply cramming their shops with all kinds of ill-assorted detritus, rather like the mismatched objects certain individuals accumulated in their own homes, sometimes displaying them on plaster plinths. The antiquarian of this period prided himself on his expertise in the history of different styles. Many examples of such characters can be found in contemporary literature – including the uncle of Beatrix in Balzac's novel of that name, the principal character in Walter Scott's *The Antiquary*, the main character in Balzac's *Peau de chagrin* and Peyrhorade in Mérimée's short story *La Vénus de l'Ille*.

It would, however, be wrong to suppose that this emphasis on style, provenance and history might have proved detrimental to the presence of plaster. In reality, during this same period, plaster acquired a certain nobility because of its use in the residences of the elite, especially in the major cities. From that time on, inside residential buildings with their carefully plastered internal walls and decorative mouldings, the increasingly strict designation of the various rooms facilitated the presence of ancient objects acquired from antique dealers and displayed in glass cases or on cushions, alongside ornaments of lesser value. All of this meant that plaster was still very much present, as exemplified by its use in death masks, for example.

In the same period, plaster casts of objects inspired by ancient masterpieces were strategically displayed in the homes and gardens of wealthy property owners, often members of provincial learned societies, and keen to gain a reputation as antiquarians in the old sense of the term – in other words, as collectors of ancient ruins and fragments. This phenomenon would later become the target of Flaubert's scorn, evident in his description of the garden of Bouvard and Pécuchet, where pride of place was given to two plaster creations: a fake Etruscan tomb, in the form of a quadrangle in black plaster standing 6 feet high; and the statue of a woman who, in the darkness of the night, frightened visitors who had come to admire the works, all of them equally vulgar, collected by the two owners.

8

The strange case of life-casting

Let us pause for a moment to reflect on the artistic particularities of plaster, qualities much prized at a time when the material played such a significant role in many studios and drawing schools.[1] Gilbert Lascault gives a detailed account of working with plaster:

> The hands of the artists and craftsmen brush lightly over the plaster, they caress it and knead it, they mix it, soften it, rub it, scratch it, they break up the surface, they scrape it, work it and transform it. [. . .] The hands play with the sense of fullness and of emptiness [. . .], with the compact and the fluid, the dense and the light, the solid and the delicate, the colossal and the slender, the smooth and the jagged, with stability and instability, with the polished and the rough, with the glossy and the roughcast, with the pared-down and the fantastical.[2]

In artists' studios and workshops, as we have already seen, plaster was at one and the same time a material used for reproducing existing statues through the casting process, a working tool used to create a statue in another material, and 'creative plaster' when it was used as a core material in its own right. For many sculptors of the period, plaster was highly prized, whether in the form of casts or when sculpted directly. It offered them the particular advantages of 'freedom of action and very rapid results'; 'It also enabled them to add or remove elements at will, and involved close physical contact between their hands and the material.'[3] Plaster could be 'moulded, layered, scraped, stamped, polished, painted, gilded [. . .]; its texture could be simple, tender, romantic, solid, hard, fluid, shaded or coloured'.[4] Plaster had its own unique quality of light, and its texture enhanced the effects of light more than any other material.

A number of artists who worked regularly with plaster regarded the results as their finest, most life-like and most intimate works.

In artists' studios, it was common practice to make plaster casts of the naked female body. This practice was a significant factor in the all-pervasive presence of plaster at that time and triggered a unique range of emotions. The sensation of being completely encased in a soft, warm substance, often from head to foot, must indeed have been a particularly intense one.

In art schools, students devoted much of their time to sketching body parts – arms, legs, torsos were all appropriate subjects, and casts moulded directly from life were used as models. These were 'teaching casts'. We have already seen that in many artists' studios entire walls were often completely covered with such items: 'plaster écorchés stood about the room; and here and there, on shelves and tables, lay fragments of classical sculpture – torsos of antique goddesses'.[5]

Casting female limbs constituted a working practice for artists seeking to sculpt the naked body. This plaster, left white, undoubtedly produced more striking effects than any photographs taken in a later era. Before casting a head from life, the first step was to obtain the model's consent. Certain physical precautions were imposed, such as shaving off any hair or at least protecting it from the plaster by the application of an oil or grease-based product. This probably explains why life casts of female heads were relatively rare. The eyelids of a head cast from life are often exaggeratedly closed – evidence that the models were afraid of the plaster getting into their eyes.

Let us now turn our attention to what might be called 'sentimental casting'. We know that, during this period, lovers were in the habit of accompanying their letters with all sorts of different objects as proof of their affection, a practice adopted for example by Gustave Flaubert and Louise Colet. Such gestures led to an increased enthusiasm for the casting of certain body parts – the hands, in particular – which then acted as a compensation for the absence of the loved one or as a memorial after their death. These plaster mementos were a combination of sentimental fetishism and sorrowful recollection.

Very often, within these circles, the refinement and delicacy of these extremities became the focus of a zealous cult. Hands, clasped or intertwined, or frozen in a gesture of surrender, formed the centrepiece of many a private altar, acting as the reminder of a promised engagement or commemorating a successful season. More broadly, life casts of this sort were regarded as tangible proof of affection.[6]

Life casts of feet and legs were particularly prized in a period where it was not considered respectable to expose these in public. Not surprisingly, a number of fakes ended up in circulation and these were in great demand. Witness, for example, the plaster foot of a certain Rachel – real name Elisabeth-Rachel Félix – an actress who had a deeply passionate following at that time.

The increased interest in this type of casting meant that the resulting casts became part of the commercial trade in small, easily reproduced plaster objects. Plaster casts of torsos, backs and legs, either bent or extended, were sold in considerable numbers. Some specialist cast-makers sold their work on commission and even produced catalogues featuring their particular specialities. All this had significant influence on the way people thought about the body at that time. The popularity of casts depicting heads or limbs meant that it was relatively commonplace to see such body parts in isolation from the human body as a whole.[7] Life-casting is always viewed in a slightly equivocal way in that it is effectively both a disturbing mirror of reality and an unaccustomed fragmentation of the body.

Let us turn our attention to the reaction of a visitor confronted with the casts that made up the Dechaume collection – an account emphasizing *a sense of physical presence* far more powerful than any conveyed by photography:

> The visitor to the collection in the studio of Geoffroy Dechaume is immediately struck by how natural the poses seem, captured in a moment of languid sensuality, or else stretching as if on the point of coming to life. It is impos-

sible not to be astonished by the technical virtuosity of these casts, the precision of the skin texture, the *sense of presence* of the models: here muscles are tensed, there a stomach relaxes as though caught off-guard curled in a foetal position.[8]

Let us consider for a moment the emotions triggered – not in the spectator this time, but in the models themselves, trapped inside the plaster as it hardens and cools down.[9] This is plaster at its most sensual. The woman, often in the bloom of youth, 'trembles inside her cast'. So, for example, in the casts on display in the studio of Geoffroy Dechaume, 'the aureole of the breasts has hardened'. The skin is entirely covered in gooseflesh. Put briefly, the emotion experienced at skin level provokes a visual emotion and triggers empathy in the spectator. This also explains why the face of the resulting cast is often tense around the eyes and the mouth and the eyelids are closed. It is all too easy to imagine the reactions of an individual locked within the cold embrace of plaster.

In the case of a facial or full-head casting, the caster would pour plaster over the face before removing the dry mould, which often needed repairing to achieve the finished state. For anthropological casts – a subject we shall be returning to – changes would often be made to the finished mask.

The magic of the plaster cast lay in its ability to produce an incredibly life-like result, capable of inducing a 'physical shiver' which was not provoked by other forms of sculpture. It was as though the gooseflesh of the young woman inside the cast in turn triggered a similar physical sensation in the spectator; the shiver of the model in reaction to being encased in the cast was somehow perfectly preserved in the plaster. 'This cannot be faked. It is something that simply happens and can very quickly be transformed into a deep sense of unease.'

Such sensations, experienced both by the body inside the cast and by the spectator, have been subject to detailed analysis.[10] The model, under the effect of the plaster, 'experiences a mild sense of anxiety triggered by the sensation of being unable to move and by a feeling of claustrophobia'. 'The living texture of the mould process coexists with a material which is inanimate, white, capable of covering everything and no longer offering any plasticity or any possibility of metamorphosis.' All of this gives rise to a feeling 'of troubling strangeness' in the presence of this embrace of 'the feminine and the neutral'. The casting process does not in fact require air, but relies simply on the contact of plaster and skin. During this invisible process, the onlooker, whether the caster or the spectator, remains on the outside and cannot experience the sensations involved. The range of emotions experienced during the casting 'mimics death'.

Casts were also made of male bodies. In this context, let us turn to the account of a spectator, dated 1854:

I cannot describe the range of my emotions during this process. First the body was placed in a seated position. A young man placed his hand on the man's head, so as to hold it in position, while oil was rubbed into his face. This young man had recently returned from Italy. He spoke of the great artists, of Michelangelo, Machiavelli, etc. As he spoke, he continued to make vigorous gestures and you could see the body being moved from side to side. It was a terrifying sight to see those closed eyes, that pale face, that final determined expression, like the mast of a ship tossed about by the waves and I found the whole spectacle profoundly disturbing. Then, plaster was applied to the face, as though one material replicated another, this expressionless white mass, this body covered by the shirt all seemed somehow still very real. Finally, the mask was removed, the jaw slackened and the mouth seemed to cry out: 'I have been through some terrible moments.'[11]

For all the reasons cited here, life-casting was the target of a great deal of criticism, particularly during the 1840s. It was not regarded as art since the artist had no active role in the process, an argument taken up by Balzac in The Unknown Masterpiece. Many critics saw the practice as little more than a menial task which lay outside the realm of fine art. In their view, plaster was incapable of capturing the profound truth of the subject and could only convey its inanimate appearance.

Life-casting was not, however, confined simply to the production of sentimental casts or models for sculptors. It was also used in three other domains: anthropology, botanical studies and medicine.

We will touch only briefly on anthropological casting here, given that in this context the role of plaster is very similar to the one we have already examined above. It was common practice at the time for explorers to make casts of the heads of indigenous peoples and to bring the plaster casts back with them on their return. In most cases, these casts were painted so as to provide a more accurate portrait but the first step in the process was, of course, to persuade potential subjects to participate in the casting process. Perhaps not surprisingly, some of them expressed a certain amount of reticence about taking part. Others expressed their reluctance to sacrifice or spoil their hair, or refused to hand over the skulls of their dead. The scholar responsible for making the mould carefully labelled each one to indicate the 'species', gender and 'place of origin' of the model.

The phrenologist[12] Alexandre Dumontier accompanied Jules Dumont d'Urville on a number of his expeditions. During the course of some of these, he made a series of casts of the Iowa Indians. Needless to say, the models were given payment of some kind. Academic institutions encouraged Dumont d'Urville to also make casts of torsos, arms and legs in order to provide a more complete picture of the physiques of indigenous peoples.

All of this was part of the explorer's work during these expeditions. As well as making life casts, cranial measurements were often recorded, and the two processes were used in the classification of human groups, a practice very much in vogue at that time. Sometimes, ethnographic sculptures were brought back along with the painted plaster models.

Life-casting was not only confined to human subjects. Many sculptors took moulds of animals and plants and the resulting plaster casts flooded onto the market. Given the importance accorded to plant forms in art at that time, this type of plaster model was extremely useful to artists.

Those making such moulds generally preferred to work on animals that either were already dead or had been stunned or chloroformed, since, unlike human subjects, it was difficult to get an animal to keep still. Making moulds of plants required very specific techniques which had been known to artists since the end of the Middle Ages. The mould was made using a paint-brush and the plants were then covered with a series of thin layers of very liquid plaster.

But the scientific use of plaster was by no means confined to the fields of anthropology or botanical studies. During the period in question, it was also widely used in the medical sector. Making moulds and creating casts from human bodies, living or dead, was considered by a great many specialists – and, in particular, by phrenologists – as an indispensable tool for expanding their understanding of mankind.

There would not be sufficient space here to examine the theories formulated by François-Joseph Gall – who died in 1828 – and those of his followers, who claimed to be able to identify the characteristics of an individual by examining the shape of his or her skull. This practice explains the immense collections of plaster models created by phrenologists. Gall's staunchest follower, for example, amassed a collection of 800–900 skulls, and the English phrenologist John D. Holm collected almost 400 plaster heads. At the same time, the Phrenological Society of Paris, created on 16 April 1831, had a collection of between 200 and 300 casts of heads. Other societies, in Rouen, Lyon or Montpellier, collected casts of heads and brains, since scholars were interested in the convolutions of this organ. A new development involved the casting of the whole head of an individual, including the brain, a process which was regarded as a significant innovation in the history of body casting.

The importance of phrenology in the history of casting, and therefore of plaster, cannot be emphasized enough. This science – for at the time it was regarded as such – meant that moulds and casts were on an equal footing with the products of ancient and modern statuary. It is also worth noting that the growing interest in phrenology coincided with the introduction and use of dissection casts in the teaching of anatomy.

According to practitioners of phrenology, the use of casts would lead to significant social developments and would allow scholars to compare the traits of criminals, artists and the sick, as well as those associated with aberrant phenomena in nature. The practice of making casts of patients afflicted with a range of different illnesses would continue throughout the entire century, and a number of major nosological collections were established as a result. Medicine was fascinated by how realistic the moulds were – for example, in the case of casts made of dermatological conditions.

The cast collection at the Hôpital Saint-Louis is still the most fascinating testimony of this era. It demonstrates the extent to which it was possible to know everything about symptoms even though the causes were not yet fully understood. The age of plaster was the combination of a craving for knowledge and a culture of organized ignorance. A vast ocean of useless speculation compensated for what was not yet known.

9

Crumbling political regimes

And now we come to the very heart of the matter. In this first half of the nineteenth century, plaster was at one and the same time a chronotype, a symbol of the past eras which it recreated through the casting process, of fragility and therefore of the crumbling, of the ephemeral, but also of the hollow and of the cheap and vulgar. Could such symbolism also apply to the political sphere in France at a time when it was manifestly impossible to create anything solid and durable – when the hollow and the crumbling seemed omnipresent? Could it epitomize a period where, in this domain as in so many others, all eyes seemed to be turned to the past, a past that people wanted to see replayed in a speeded-up version since, for so many of them, the Revolution had brought with it the experience of a suddenly accelerated timescale.

Hartog refers to 'The nineteenth century's self-representation as the century of the historian – understood as the memory of what is no longer and the harbinger of what is yet to come.'[1] In his description, the early years of the century can be seen as a moment of indecision for the future of politics, no longer illuminated by a solid past.

The symbolic role of plaster can be compared to that of the metal girder and of plastic in the two periods which were to follow, and indeed, in the case of England, to the role played by coal in a country that had not experienced political revolution for a very long time and where a stable regime remained in place.

Let us turn our attention first of all to the so-called 'July' monarchy. In doing so, we have, of course, no intention of rewriting the history of that period. A great number of excellent books have been written on this subject since David Pinkney – now some considerable time ago – offered his detailed analysis of the 1830 revolution and Michael Marrinan turned his attention to the notion of self-presentation as devised and set in place by Louis-Philippe.[2]

After the Restoration – an era of rubble, debris and ruins, which had of necessity shouldered the burden of reassembling the scattered fragments in so many different domains – the July Monarchy heralded the start of a new era. It introduced the era of the hollow, of the ephemeral, of a politics moulded on the past. From that point on, and with ever more force, plaster increasingly symbolized the essence of the crumbling, fragile nature of politics. The political fragility of the regime and of the king, so often under threat; the replastering effort in the form of the so-called 'hastily put-together' Charter; the care devoted to restoring the monuments of the past; the fascination, and sometimes nostalgia, triggered by past centuries – all emphasize this parallel with plaster. All of these elements are symbolized in the work of Victor Hugo, with the juxtaposition of solid Gothic stone and the hollow interior of the Bastille elephant.

Let us sketch out some of the elements that make it possible to describe the July Monarchy as a regime of plaster. In a process very much akin to replastering, the founding text, the Charter of 14 August 1830, reproduces the texts of the Charter proclaimed by Louis XVIII in 1814, at the time of his accession to the throne. Drawn up over the course of just five days, the new Charter is a simple contract made between the king and the nation. It ended the notion of state religion and abandoned any reference to Divine Providence, which would have favoured the return of Louis XVIII. That aside, the text consists of a number of elements borrowed from the English system. Essentially, it amounted to a collection of memories and of imitations hastily replastered. And it was only by 219 votes out of the 406 deputies – of whom only 259 attended the session on that day – that the Chamber agreed to bestow royalty on the Duke of Orléans, making him Louis-Philippe I. Consequently, therefore, no formal coronation took place, just a simple oath sworn on the Charter by the king of the French in the presence of the members of the Palais-Bourbon.

Yet this was not the most important aspect of the period. Throughout his reign, the king's life was constantly under threat, symbolizing the essential fragility even of the sovereign. Not only was there the terrible assassination attempt masterminded by Fieschi in 1835, in which eighteen people were killed and twenty-two injured, but there was also a series of subsequent ones, all of which contributed to a growing climate of uncertainty. After a period of some three years during which he travelled throughout France in order to meet the French people, fear of further assassination attempts forced Louis-Philippe to abandon this means of consolidating his popularity. In this context, his decision in 1840 not to participate in the procession and festivities marking the erection of the Bastille column commemorating the 'Three glorious days' is clearly significant. On the day in question, a long procession made its way across the capital, but the king chose to remain in his palace, from where he could wave as it passed, an indication that he had begun to question both his own legitimacy and that of his regime, already challenged in 1832 by the popular uprising so vividly described by Victor Hugo in *Les Misérables*, and saved only by a decisive massacre. All of this reflected the impossibility of creating anything solid.

Many historians have been dismissive of the caricature drawn by Charles Philipon in 1831 in which the king's face was depicted as a pear. In reality, this image carried considerable symbolic weight, going well beyond the small gestures of insurrection made by school students rebelling against the symbols of their institution.

Let us recall the figurine evoked in the portrait of Cousin Pons. The pear, representing the monarch in all his vulgarity, constituted an element of his fragility.[3]

Yet the fragile nature of the Orleanist dynasty was not the only characteristic it shared with plaster. The July Monarchy was the regime which set most store by history and the past. This period saw the transition from conservation to restoration, with the creation of institutions that would facilitate the drawing up of an inventory of historic monuments – very often medieval ones – deemed worthy of restoration, a process in which Mérimée played a key role.[4] As a result, plaster was increasingly in demand for making casts and reconstructing missing fragments in order to restore the damaged statues of the most famous monuments. It temporarily saved an ancient art, an echo of this monarchy reinstated with such difficulty in a contemporary world which regarded it with hostility.

Thanks to his trips around France, organized by Baron Taylor to explore the picturesque and romantic aspects of the country, and his support of the doctrine espoused by Viollet-le-Duc, Mérimée succeeded in imposing his views on the restoration of ancient monuments. For him the important thing was never simply to reproduce the past, however beautiful it might be. He advocated a modest approach and was suspicious of misplaced restoration. He focused his attention on compiling inventories of monuments worthy of restoration and, if possible, ensured they could be saved by relying on tangible evidence, the essential aim being to conserve what already existed. This mode of restoration thrived under the July Monarchy, until Viollet-le-Duc determined to let buildings tell their own story, even if it was one that had never been told, an approach that resulted in the past being made more beautiful than it had ever been in reality.

Yet this is not all, since the king himself – as though in compensation for his failure to take his place on the royal stage – was determined to celebrate the glory of France's past, and to do so across a variety of settings and in different ways.

Much has been written on the Gallery of Great Battles commissioned by Louis-Philippe in the Palace of Versailles – a celebration and a reminder of heroic times, in which plaster had no role. But it has often been somewhat overlooked that, in this same palace, on 10 June 1837, he inaugurated a gallery of plaster statues representing the great figures of French history, most of which were made by François-Henri Jaquet between 1835 and 1846. In 1850, this gallery housed 342 plaster statues. These were the result of operations carried out both in the French provinces and abroad. So, for example, a cast of the tomb of the Duke of Montpensier was made in Westminster Abbey in 1835, whilst others were produced in Bruges or Granada. In addition, Louis-Philippe commissioned new casts from the Louvre workshops.

The year 1844 saw the opening of the Cluny Museum destined to house the medieval collections assembled by Alexandre du Sommerard. The inauguration of the museum coincided with a time when the arts of the Middle Ages were the subject of intense fascination but were still largely under-represented in official institutions, with little space devoted to them in museums. In 1833, François Guizot founded the Société de l'histoire de France, chaired by Prosper de Barante, the historian whose work ranged from the history of the dukes of Burgundy to the Empire of Napoleon III.

Under the July Monarchy, historians such as Adolphe Thiers, initially, and Guizot in particular (under the symbolic guidance of Marshal Soult) exercised considerable power. During the same period, Jules Michelet, professor at the Collège de France, had started to write his historical texts, and Alphonse de Lamartine, a successful historian, was warning the Palais-Bourbon of the dangers of a revolution founded on contempt.

From deep within the heart of the country, there were other indications of the taste for – and even, in some cases, new fascination with – the atmosphere of the past and the exploits of great men. The Scottish writer Walter Scott, who had so magnificently depicted the twelfth and thirteenth centuries in Great Britain, was widely read and admired in France, especially since *Quentin Durward*, one of his greatest novels, was set in the reign of Louis XI, the most intriguing monarch in French history. It was under the July Monarchy that Dumas published *The Three Musketeers*, and Alfred de Vigny wrote several of his historical novels, including *Cinq Mars*. It was a period when paintings of historical subjects triumphed in the artistic Salons, and these continued to be reproduced in high-quality reference works until the middle of the twentieth century.

Plaster, in the various ways we have seen above, facilitated this desire to look back on the past, but it also haunted the imagination as a symbol of the hollow.[5] When Victor Hugo published *Les Misérables*, readers found themselves confronted with the intriguing spectacle of the Bastille elephant, destined to be caught up in the events of the 1832 insurrection.

By the time of these events, just two years after the introduction of the July Monarchy, the elephant – which, according to Hugo, was originally commissioned by Napoleon I at the very end of his reign – had become an imposing but hollow monster, and was destined to be replaced two years later by the Bastille column. With the combination of plaster and hollow space, the elephant was clearly highly symbolic in the mind of the author. The hollow monster represented the inability to create anything solid in this first half of the nineteenth century and is such a powerful presence in the novel that, for the reader, the grandiose appearance of the sculpture is inextricably associated with the plaster and hollow space of its construction.

Let us turn to Victor Hugo, who points out that the Bastille elephant – the imposing maquette he refers to as 'a vast carcass of an idea of Napoleon'[6] – was in fact nothing more than 'a rough model'.[7] In 1832, according to the novelist, it 'had become historical, and had acquired a definiteness which contrasted with its provisional aspect'.[8] In this way, according to Hugo, the plaster model, standing between the prison and the column, represented one of the three elements of the history of the Bastille.

Yet, it is worth emphasizing that this structure was indeed a plaster 'model', a symbol of the temporary and therefore the ephemeral. When Gavroche lived in it, the elephant was 'falling into ruin; every season, the mortar which was detached from its sides made hideous wounds upon it'.[9] The elephant 'was in a hollow', Hugo added, for the earth was sinking under its weight, just as the July Monarchy, a regime symbolized by the hollow, would soon collapse in its turn.

'The architect of the elephant had succeeded in making something grand with plaster; the architect of the stove-pipe [the Bastille column] has succeeded in making something petty with bronze.'[10] Put briefly, the plaster model destined to be remade in bronze was a harbinger of the greatness of a regime: the Empire. Hugo then turns his attention back to the plaster version: 'Above, a long dusty beam, from which projected at regular distances massive encircling timbers, represented the vertical column with its ribs, stalactites of plaster hung down like the viscera.'[11]

Inside the elephant, Gavroche 'felt beneath his feet a terrible disaggregation',[12] a sense of fragility which, for Hugo, symbolized the precarious beginnings of the July Monarchy: 'so newly set up, and so far from secure'.[13]

It is not our intention here to claim that the Second Republic was made of plaster, that it was hollow and crumbling. To do so would risk overstating the analogy. But it is clear to everyone that this ephemeral regime, haunted by history, re-enacted the Revolution which remained omnipresent in people's memories. The Second Republic was a succession of patterns echoing the episodes of the first one, as though this earlier period were simply being repeated. Lamartine, whose *Histoire des Girondins* had been a huge success at the end of the July Monarchy, was all too aware of this phenomenon and continually referred to it throughout the events of 1848.

The new regime emerged from the ruins of a constitutional monarchy with the establishment of a moderate republic, as in 1792, but its provisional government was very soon eclipsed by a delegation of five members – a sort of new Directory – which quickly collapsed under the dictatorship of Cavaignac, after a second decisive massacre. This was followed by a period of two years of temporary equilibrium thanks to the November Constitution and the election of a president by universal suffrage, which, in December, conferred power on a Bonaparte who would go on to reinstate the Empire in two separate stages and by means of two plebiscites.

It is widely acknowledged that these turbulent events would end up replaying on a global scale an accelerated version of the history of France as it had unfolded, fifty years earlier, from the summer of 1792 to 1804. And it would take too long and be too far from our subject here to list all the stages involved in this process of recollecting and revisiting the past, which would ultimately present the people of the time with a series of crumbling political moulds.

Then, even before the beginning of the 1860s, France witnessed the first signs of the era of the metal girder and the metal-framed construction. The Baltard Pavilion, based on designs drawn up by the president-prince at the end of 1851, was constructed shortly afterwards and many market halls were erected in smaller French towns. At the same time, a major rail network was being constructed. During the same period, this symbolic transfer continued to be reflected in the policies relating to public works, subsequently studied by Louis Girard.[14] It is worth remembering, however, that plaster, in a kind of overlapping of material chronotypes, found itself put to more noble uses in the facades and interiors of Haussman's Paris – as demonstrated by the stucco, staff, mouldings and smooth partition walls which contributed to the enhancement of private life in the apartments of the elite.

This shift towards the metal girder brings to an end the history of a time when plaster was very much in the forefront of the popular imagination as a result of its omnipresence in construction work, in the restoration of monuments, in artistic techniques, in aesthetics, in a growing sensitivity to death and in the taste for sentimental mementos. Not forgetting, of course, its symbolic role in the political domain under the Restoration, and even more so under the July Monarchy – the very model of a hollow regime – and subsequently under the Second

Republic, with the sheer weight of history and successive remouldings of the past.

In 1889, the Eiffel Tower would stamp its indelible mark on the era of a triumphant Republic.

Notes

History: from stone to plastic

1 Edgar Morin, *Commune en France: la métamorphose de Plozévet*, Paris: Fayard, 1967.

1 The half-century of plaster

1 The philosopher Alain, real name Emilie August Chartier, 1868–1951 published his daily 'propos' (philosophical remarks) in local newspapers.

2 Alain, *Propos*, Paris: Gallimard, 1970, vol. II: *Propos* from March 1925, p. 665.

3 The French term used here, 'bric-à-bracolage', comes from, and was probably first used in, Balzac's *Cousin Pons*. Translator's note: in the English translation, this becomes 'the bric-à-brac confraternity': Honoré de Balzac, *Cousin Pons*, London: Penguin, 1968, p. 26.

4 Expression borrowed from a chapter heading in A. Corbin, *The Foul and the Fragrant: Odor and the French Social Imagination*, Leamington Spa, Hamburg, New York: Berg Publishers, 1986, p. 161.

5 The French expression *essuyer les plâtres* refers to
the fact that prostitutes were often the first inhab-
itants of newly plastered buildings. They would
therefore literally 'wipe down' the fresh plaster with
their clothes. Once the plaster was dry, these unfortunate tenants would be forced to leave and higher
rents could be imposed. In French, the expression
has come to mean trying something out for the first
time, or having to face teething problems.
6 François Hartog, *Regimes of Historicity: Presentism
and Experiences of Time*, New York: Columbia
University Press, 2015.
7 Victor Hugo, *Les Misérables*, Ware: Wordsworth
Editions, 1994.
8 Victor Hugo, *The Hunchback of Notre-Dame*,
London: Richard Bentley, 1833, p. 126.

2 Plaster houses and poverty

1 François Hartog, *Regimes of Historicity: Presentism
and Experiences of Time*, New York: Columbia
University Press, 2015.
2 See note 5 in chapter 1.
3 Morel, cited by Jacques Hantraye, 'Essuyer les plâtres', *La Lettre blanche* (Paris: Musée du Plâtre),
no. 52, April 2015, p. 4.
4 These were prostitutes registered with the *préfecture
de police* in Paris, or with the offices of the munici-
pal police in the provinces.
5 See Hantraye, 'Essuyer les plâtres', p. 5.
6 Cited by Vincent Farion, 'Le plâtre changé en or, l'or
changé en plâtre: les mots et les images, symboles
de richesse', in Ada Aconvitsioti-Hameau, Philippe
Hameau and Martin de la Soudière (eds.), 'L'or

blanc: de la métaphor des sens à la réalité environne-mentale et économique', supplement 15 to *Cahier de l'Aser*, 2020; Honoré de Balzac, *History of the Thirteen*, London: Penguin Books, 1974, p. 64.

7 Honoré de Balzac, *A Harlot High and Low*, London: Penguin, 1985, cited in Farion, 'Le plâtre changé en or', p. 44.

8 Honoré de Balzac, *Histoire et physiologie des boule-vards de Paris* (1945), cited by Farion, 'Le plâtre changé en or', p. 43.

9 Balzac, *Histoire et physiologie des boulevards de Paris*.

10 Honoré de Balzac, *Le Père Goriot*, Oxford University Press, 1999, p. 128.

11 Honoré de Balzac, *The Duchesse de Langeais*, Boston: Roberts Brothers, 1885, p. 198, cited by Farion, 'Le plâtre changé en or', p. 42.

12 Balzac, *Père Goriot*, p. 1.

13 Honoré de Balzac, *Beatrix*, London: J. M. Dent, 1896, p. 275.

14 Honoré de Balzac, *The Brotherhood of Consolation: Z. Marcas*, Boston: Roberts Brothers, 1896, p. 336.

15 Balzac, *Père Goriot*, p. 118.

16 Farion, 'Le plâtre changé en or', p. 47.

3 Restoring ancient monuments

1 Hugo is referring to the Théatre de l'Ambigu-Comique on the Boulevard du Temple in Paris, which was rebuilt after a fire in 1828.

2 Victor Hugo, *Voyages*, Paris: Robert Laffont, 1987, pp. 602–4.

3 Ibid., pp. 18–19.

4 Ibid., p. 22.

5 Ibid., p. 531.

6 This phrase, 'temps des prothèses', was the title of an essay in the exhibition catalogue *Le Corps en morceaux* (English title: 'The dislocated body') at the Musée d'Orsay in 1990. The essay title refers to the debate over whether or not to 'complete' torsos by replacing missing limbs, etc.

7 Geneviève Bresc-Bautier, 'Temps des prothèses, avant l'âge de la restauration', in *Le Corps en morceaux*, Paris: Réunion des musées nationaux, 1990, pp. 79–85.

8 Ibid.

9 Sophie Lagabrielle, 'Mouler, créer: l'utilisation des moulages dans les restaurations des monuments au XIX siècle', in Georges Barthe (ed.), *Le Plâtre: l'art et la matière*, Paris: Éditions Créaphis, 2002, pp. 119–28.

10 Ibid., p. 119.

11 Ibid., p. 120.

12 Jannie Mayer, 'L'utilisation du plâtre dans un grand chantier de restauration au XIX siècle: la cathédrale Notre-Dame de Paris', in Barthe (ed.), *Le Plâtre*, pp. 129–36 and, in particular, p. 133.

13 Lagabrielle, 'Mouler, créer', p. 123.

4 Plaster: allegory of a phantom century

1 François-René de Chateaubriand, *Memoirs from beyond the Tomb*, London: Penguin, 2014, p. xvi.

2 François Hartog, *Regimes of Historicity: Presentism and Experiences of Time*, New York: Columbia University Press, 2015.

3 Alain Corbin, 'La nécessité de l'assemblage', in *Une histoire des sens*, Paris: Robert Laffont, 2016, pp. 581–92.

4 On the subject of this atmosphere and the proliferation of ruins, see the work of Emmanuel Fureix, especially Emmanuel Fureix (ed.), *Iconoclasme et révolutions*, Paris: Éditions Champ Vallon, 2014.

5 Alfred de Musset, *The Confession of a Child of the Century*, London: Penguin, 2013, p. 10.

6 Ibid.

7 Ibid., pp. 19–20.

8 Ibid., p. 31 [author's italics].

9 Ibid., p. 75.

10 Translator's note: the author is citing the expression *défaut d'être* which he has used earlier in the book (p. 4). This expression – translated as 'a sense of a flawed existence' – is a reference to Musset's own generation and the beginning of the Romantic movement, when young people felt a sense of disenchantment and of disillusionment in the face of so many recent political and historical upheavals.

11 For more detailed information on all these points, see S. Michaud, A. Corbin and P. Georgel, *L'invention du XIX siècle*, Paris: Éditions Klincksieck, 2002.

5 **Plaster casts and the art of the hollow**

1 For more on the history of casting, see *Actes des rencontres internationales sur les moulages*, Éditions de l'Université de Montpellier III, 2000.

2 F. Rionnet, *L'Atelier de moulage du musée du Louvre (1794–1928)*, Paris: Réunion des musées nationaux, collection 'Notes et documents des musées de France', 28, 1996, p. 410. This publica-

tion constitutes a genuine bible for the history of artistic casts, techniques, people, ethics, commercial distribution, teaching of drawing, establishment of plaster museums, etc.

3 Ibid., pp. 34ff.
4 Ibid.
5 Ibid., pp. 39ff.
6 Ibid., pp. 57ff.
7 Ibid., pp. 64ff.
8 As described in ibid.
9 Ibid., p. 92.
10 Ibid., pp. 67ff.

6 Immortalizing the dead in plaster

1 Marie-Pierre Rinck, *Le Plâtre: empreinte, moulage, décoration*, Paris: Fleurus, 1987. On the subject of the techniques used, see Emmanuelle Héran (ed.), *Le Dernier Portrait*, Paris: Réunion des musées nationaux, 2002.
2 Alain Pougetoux, 'Le Masque de Napoléon: de la relique au bibelot', in Héran (ed.), *Le Dernier Portrait*.
3 Héran (ed.), *Le Dernier Portrait*, pp. 26ff. and pp. 53–7.
4 Ibid., pp. 50–3.
5 On all these points, see the work of Bruno Bertherat.
6 For more on what follows, see Héran (ed.), *Le Dernier Portrait*, pp. 80ff.
7 The *Manuels Roret* were a series of manuals published from 1822 to 1939 that offered advice on a whole range of subjects, including science, art, culture and crafts.
8 Gustave Flaubert, *The Letters of Gustave Flaubert 1830–1857*, Cambridge, MA and London: Harvard

University Press, 1980, p. 38. The letter cited was written on 25 March 1846.

9 With reference to Géricault's death mask, its construction, its distribution and the discussion and emotional turmoil it provoked, see Bruno Chenique, 'Le masque de Géricault ou la folle mémoire d'un culte sentimental et nauséabond', in Héran (ed.), *Le Dernier Portrait*, pp. 158–74.

10 Ibid., p. 166.

11 See Pougetoux, 'Le Masque de Napoléon'.

12 Longwood was the final residence of Napoleon Bonaparte.

7 Ornaments and figurines: plaster within the home

1 On this subject, see Manuel Charpy, 'Accumulation et voisinage dans les intérieurs parisiens du XIX siècle', in Valérie Gaillard (ed.), *Boulimie d'objets: l'être et l'avoir dans nos sociétés*, Paris: De Boeck Supérieure, 2014, pp. 65–89.

2 Alfred de Musset, *The Confession of a Child of the Century*, London: Penguin, 2013, p. 31.

3 For further reading, see Aude Déruelle (ed.), *Honoré de Balzac: Le cousin Pons*, Presses universitaires de Rennes, 2018 – especially M. Charpy, 'Le temps en provision: Pons et l'économie de la curiosité dans le Paris des années 1840', pp. 225–49.

4 Honoré de Balzac, *Cousin Pons*, London: Penguin Books, 1968, pp. 19–22.

5 The character of the antique dealer had already appeared in England (Walter Scott, *The Antiquary*, London: Longman, Hurst, Rees, Orme and Brown, 1816).

8 The strange case of life-casting

1 E. Papet (ed.), *À fleur de peau: le moulage sur nature au XIXème siècle*, Paris: Réunion des musées nationaux, 2001.

2 G. Lascault, 'Métamorphoses du plâtre', in Georges Barthe (ed.), *Le Plâtre: l'art et la matière*, Paris: Éditions Créaphis, 2002.

3 G. Lacroix, 'Réalité caché ou les dessous de la matière', in Barthe (ed.), *Le Plâtre*, p. 227.

4 Ibid. See also Lascault, 'Métamorphoses du plâtre'.

5 Honoré de Balzac, *The Unknown Masterpiece*, London: J. M. Dent and Co., 1896, p. 4.

6 *Le Corps en morceaux* (exhibition catalogue), Paris: Réunion des musées nationaux, 1990.

7 Georges Didi-Huberman, 'L'air et l'empreinte', in Papet (ed.), *À fleur de peau*, pp. 46–8.

8 Ibid.

9 Ibid.

10 Philippe Sorel, 'La phrénologie et le moulage', in Papet (ed.), *À fleur de peau*, pp. 106–7.

11 This text is an extract from the writings of the sculptor David d'Angers (1788–1856). It was written in 1854.

12 A phrenologist studies the shape and size of the human skull in order to identify character traits.

9 Crumbling political regimes

1 F. Hartog, *Regimes of Historicity: Presentism and Experiences of Time*, New York: Columbia University Press, 2015, p. 83.

2 D. Pinkney, *The French Revolution of 1830*, New Jersey: Princeton University Press, 1972;

M. Marrinan, *Painting Politics for Louis-Philippe*, New Haven: Yale University Press, 1988.

3 F. Erre, *Le Règne de la Poire: caricatures de l'esprit bourgeois de Louis-Philippe à nos jours*, Paris: Éditions Champ Vallon, 2011.

4 For further detail on this point, see André Fermigier, 'Mérimée et l'inspection des monuments historiques', in P. Nora (ed.), *Les Lieux de mémoire*, Paris: Gallimard, 1973 and 1995, vol. II, pp. 281–3 and 287.

5 P. Bellanger, 'De la commercialité du plâtre', in Georges Barthe (ed.), *Le Plâtre: l'art et la matière*, Paris: Éditions Créaphis, 2002, p. 196.

6 Victor Hugo, *Les Misérables*, Ware: Wordsworth Editions, 1994, p. 651.

7 Ibid.

8 Ibid.

9 Ibid.

10 Ibid., p. 652.

11 Ibid., p. 654.

12 Ibid., p. 576.

13 Ibid., p. 573.

14 L. Girard, *La Politique des travaux publics sous le Second Empire*, Paris: Colin, 1952.